From Jesus with Love

FOR TROUBLED TIMES

Compiled and edited by Maria Fontaine

Design by Giselle LeFavre and Doug Calder

ISBN # 3-03730-147-3

© 2003 Aurora Production AG, Switzerland

Printed in Malaysia by Rhythm

www.auroraproduction.com

Contents

INTRODUCTION

This book of messages from Jesus contains many wonderful assurances that He will help us through those trying times when we most need His love and comfort. Jesus has a solution for every problem and can bring us through any trouble. Nothing is too difficult for Him. He can also bring about marvelous changes in us in the process.

Jesus has said that these messages are His promises to His children. Like gold coins and jewels in a treasure chest, they are there for us to pull out and redeem whenever we need them. As we claim those promises as our own, He will keep His word and honor our faith. He will go to work on our problems, and we will be rewarded, encouraged, strengthened, and transformed.

That's the key to overcoming troubles—faith. When we have the unshakable conviction that Jesus loves us and is going to take care of us no matter what, even the seemingly impossible becomes possible. Often our first reaction to troubles is just the opposite—a feeling of defeat, discouragement, and depression—but Jesus wants us to be helped and happy, not defeated and discouraged. That's why He tells us repeatedly how much He wants us to turn to Him in times of trouble and to rest in His arms in times of weakness. When we do, He takes our loads and helps us with our problems.

So when you find yourself in the midst of troubles, let Jesus tell you how He sees things. As you get His perspective, your faith will grow. Then you'll be ready to take the next step of faith by following the counsel He gives. Day by day as you stay in close communication with Him, you'll find that place of perfect peace in Him and He will be able to bring you through any trouble victoriously.

I care for you

My love

My love is patient and understanding in a world of intolerance. My love is tender and kind when people are callous or indifferent. My love comforts in times of sorrow. My love consoles the lonely. My love brings clarity of mind to those who are confused, rest to the weary, help to the helpless, and renewed strength to those who feel they can't go on. My love brings peace in the midst of life's storms.

My love can heal broken bodies. It can even soothe and mend broken hearts. My love melts away tension, worry, and strain. My love gives faith and courage in place of fear, hope in place of despair. My love is light and drives away the darkness. My love will descend to any depth to save, go to any length to rescue. My love knows no stopping place. There is no problem that My love can't overcome.

My love is My special gift to you. It has always been there for you, and always will be. Won't you take it now?

Connect with Me

No matter what your circumstances or how you have handled them up till now, no matter what you have done or not done, I love you. I see your every tear. I hear your every cry for help. I feel your every heartache, your every sorrow, your every frustration, your every worry. I know your every desire. I see straight through to your heart of hearts and all that is in it, and I love you more deeply than you can possibly comprehend.

I see your struggles and I want to help. Life is often a struggle, but it is made so much easier when you spiritually connect with Me. I have all the love and comfort and peace and solutions you seek. I am right here at your side, waiting patiently for you to reach out to Me so I can relieve your troubled mind, dry your tears, and show you how much I love you.

Through the storm

I can't promise to spare you from the storms of life, but I can promise to be with you through them. My help comes in a variety of forms. It may not always come in the form you expect, but it will come. I will never leave you to struggle on your own.

When you ask for My help, I will answer your prayer. When you are fearful, I will give you faith to trust Me, peace of mind, and courage to go on. When you are weak and weary, lean on Me and I will give you strength like you've never known. When your heart is broken, I will mend it.

I can't keep you from all hardships and sorrows, but I can make the troubles of life bearable and bring about good in the end. I can help your spirit rise above the storms of life. Above the clouds—up here in heavenly places with Me—the sun is always shining. I am sunshine on a rainy day, the rainbow after the storm. I am the bright ray of hope that puts the sparkle back in your eyes.

The present storm will pass. In the meantime, let Me keep you through the storm.

6

Meet Me in the morning

You do well to take time with Me first thing in the morning, for you are powerless without the strength you draw from Me, you are foolish without the wisdom you learn from Me, and you have no love to share with others unless you first get it from Me. Without Me, you would continue on in your own little world and be limited to your own meager resources. Your human strength would run out before the day had scarcely started, your own thoughts would get in the way, and you wouldn't go far on yesterday's store of love. But when you come to Me, I open the boundless world of My Spirit to you. I am wisdom, I am strength, and I am love.

Haven't I said in My Word that you must labor in order to enter into My rest? (Hebrews 4:11 KJV). It seems easier to carry on in your own energy than to work at entering into the realm of My Spirit where I would carry you along, but that's not so; you really make it harder for yourself, because you make it harder for Me to help you.

So take a little time each morning to hear from Me and enter into My rest. Practice makes perfect. As you practice reaching out to Me, it will become easier. Keep taking this time with Me each morning, and I will be here for you.

Only believe

How faith works

If faith no larger than a mustard seed can move a mountain (Matthew 17:20), you figure that your faith must be small indeed, because your prayers seem to go unanswered. That can be disheartening, I know, but it shouldn't stop you from asking Me for a miracle when you need one.

There are a couple of things you should know about faith: First, it's not something you can earn or muster up yourself, but it's a gift from your heavenly Father. Second, like a muscle, faith needs nourishment and exercise to grow. That spiritual nourishment comes from reading and absorbing God's Word. You exercise your faith by acting on it. So nourish and put your faith to work daily through your prayers and actions.

You don't have to wait till you feel you have strong faith to begin receiving My help, though. If you need results now but feel you don't have enough faith to warrant them, ask Me to increase your faith. Be like the man in the Bible who begged Me to heal his son, who could not hear or speak. The man had every reason to doubt that things could ever be different, and he did. He knew that his faith was weak, so when I asked him if he believed I could heal his son he replied, "Lord, I believe. Help my unbelief." The moment he confessed his inadequacy and asked for My help, he received both faith and the miracle—his son was instantly healed!

You don't have to be perfect

A lot of people don't pray until they're in some sort of trouble, and then they find they don't have the kind of faith that gets results. Their faith is weak because it's been so long since they last exercised it, and they feel their relationship with Me is strained because they didn't place much importance on it before trouble struck. They feel hypocritical or undeserving, and don't know where to start in making things right.

It is much easier to pray full-of-faith prayers when you have a history of praying and receiving My answers, when you feel close to Me because you've opened your heart to Me day by day, and when you know you've done your best to please Me. But even if you don't meet those conditions, there's hope. You don't have to be perfect for Me to answer your prayers. I help all who call on Me in faith and humble desperation.

Simply turn to Me in your time of need, get your heart right by confessing your faults and receiving My forgiveness, believe that I can perform the miracle you need, and I will. Best of all, this can be the start of a whole new life with Me in which you experience more answers to prayers and a greater closeness to Me.

The path to victory and miracles

Praising Me brings you into My presence. It puts your spirit in close proximity to Mine, where you can feel My love and more easily see things as I see them.

Praise is the voice of faith, because when you praise Me you're acknowledging that only I am capable of solving your problems, and you're declaring that you believe I will.

Praising Me opens the door to the spiritual realm. It lifts you above circumstances in the physical realm and brings you into the land of the spirit where I'm in complete control and everything is possible.

Praise also lifts your own spirit. When you dwell on the good and speak of the good, then good surrounds you. If you start praising Me even when you don't feel like it, it lifts you up in the spirit and soon you will feel like it. I always bless and reward praise.

Praising Me even helps those around you. It lifts their spirits and encourages them. It engenders faith and trust in Me, encouragement, and positiveness.

Putting everything in My hands by praising Me increases your faith exponentially. That's a law of the spirit. It always works!

Consider the sparrow...

My eye is on the sparrow as she flutters about in search of food and a place to nest. I guide her to a resting place, and she trusts Me. She doesn't worry about what she doesn't have. She just goes about her day and trusts that I will provide her needs. How small and numerous are the sparrows, and yet I know and watch over them all. I remember and care for each one (Psalm 84:3; Matthew 6:26; 10:29).

You, My child, are far more precious to Me than all the sparrows combined, and if I show such concern for these small and seemingly insignificant birds, will I not also care for you?

I know your troubles and I understand your fears. I am here to give you faith and answer your prayers, but I need you to trust Me as the little sparrow does. You don't see her fluttering about in a panic, worried and flurried. She is calm and peaceful, knowing that My eye is on her and I will care for her as My own.

My eye is on you, too, and I stand ready to help. So trust Me, won't you? Let Me do the worrying!

Hideaway

Everyone is worried about the future these days—and it's no wonder. The way things are going, everyone has reason to fear what will happen to them, their family, their city, their country, their world. This planet has become a frightening and stressful place to live. Sometimes you wish you could find a hideaway, nail the windows and doors closed, and keep the world out.

It doesn't do any good to pretend the problems aren't there, but you don't have to be afraid, because I'm looking out for you. When fears overwhelm you, hide away in Me. When you find yourself in a dangerous situation, call on Me for help and then rest assured that I will be there to protect you. When you can't watch over your loved ones, commit them to My care. When a national or international crisis erupts, I will provide a safe haven for you and yours.

And even if the unthinkable happens—if you or your loved ones are taken from this life—know that a better life awaits on the other side. Heaven is where all this world's wrongs are made right.

So you see, although there's plenty you could worry about, you don't have to worry about a thing. I'm taking care of you!

One hurdle at a time

A hurdler must clear the hurdles one at a time. If he worries about the ones that are still many yards ahead, he is likely to lose his focus on the hurdle coming up. You can learn from him. Take your problems one at a time rather than trying to leap over all of them at once.

Let Me carry the weight

These burdens were not designed to fit on your narrow shoulders; they were intended for Me to carry. I fashioned it this way so you would realize your need for Me and draw closer to Me as you learn to depend on Me. I will carry you through if you will give all your cares to Me.

Fly to Me

As you fly to Me on the wings of prayer, as you retreat from the battlefield of the problems you struggle against to get rested and regain your spiritual strength and hear from Me, I will give you solutions that will make the problems melt away. Relief is there for you, but you must rest and lean wholly on Me.

Praise brings peace

Why endure another sleepless night? Why suffer from anxiety when you can give your cares to Me and I can give you peace of mind? Even in the bleakest circumstances, I can give you amazing peace that will relieve the mental and physical stress caused by worry and fear.

My peace comes to your heart when you turn your eyes from your troubles and toward Me. Stop worrying and think about Me. Find one thing to thank Me for—one special thing that I have done for you in the past—and praise Me for that. Or think of the worst thing that's ever happened to you and the fact that you're still here, and turn that thought into a prayer of thanksgiving. Even if you didn't pray at the time, even if you didn't yet know Me at the time, it was I who brought you through that situation. I've been watching over you your whole life, and I have either helped you through or spared you from more troubles than you can imagine—just like I'm going to help you through your present problems.

The more you praise Me, the more My peace will fill your heart.

Troubled, yet not distressed

If you think you have troubles, consider My apostle Paul: He was whipped on five occasions and beaten with rods on another. He was stoned and left for dead. He was shipwrecked three times, and spent a night and a day in the deep. He went through perils at sea, perils in the wilderness, and perils in cities. He suffered at the hands of robbers, his own countrymen, strangers, and even those who claimed to be My followers. He was imprisoned and deprived of basic needs many times (2 Corinthians 11:24–28; Acts 16:23).

Yet through all that, Paul kept trusting Me and pointing others to Me with such declarations of faith as: "We are troubled on every side, yet not distressed," and "In all these things we are more than conquerors through Him who loved us" (2 Corinthians 4:8 KJV; Romans 8:37).

Paul had great faith, yes, but don't forget that he was as human as you. He had a wonderful personal link with Me that millions since have envied, but what most people fail to realize is that this was born of the troubles that befell him. He learned to turn to Me and My Word in his time of need—and you can too.

Will you allow yourself to be distressed by present or future troubles? Or will you hold on to Me for dear life, as Paul did? I will always be there for you, as I was always there for him.

Feeling the financial squeeze

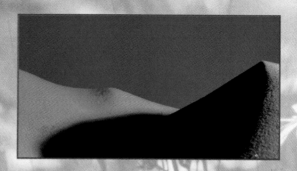

When usual means fail…

When you've done all you can and exhausted your usual means of supply but still struggle to make ends meet, don't despair; I can provide by other means. When others fail in their financial responsibilities or you are adversely affected by their wrong or selfish decisions, don't despair; I remain true and will make up for their lacks. When disaster strikes and unforeseen bills follow, don't despair; I'll pick up where your insurance policy leaves off. When the economy is tight and jobs are scarce, don't despair; I am able to supply even in impossible circumstances.

"Ask, and it will be given to you; seek, and you will find; knock, and it will be opened to you" (Matthew 7:7). That is a promise I made long ago, and it still holds true. Tell Me your needs, ask Me to supply them. Do your part—the asking, seeking, and knocking—and I will do Mine.

When you find yourself in a financial bind and don't know how to get yourself out of it, let Me get you out of it. I can supply for My children by the most unexpected and unconventional means, and I delight in doing so because I love them. It also helps them appreciate Me more when I supply, and I like that part too.

My riches are yours

The secret to obtaining both spiritual riches and material supply is actually quite simple: Realize what vast resources are at My disposal.

My Word contains hundreds of promises that are yours to claim. As you read, absorb, and claim them, you will see answers to your prayers that will thrill your soul and cause your faith to grow. And as you continue to read and absorb and claim, I will continue to answer and inspire and provide. Together we will create an unbeatable, unbreakable cycle of success.

That is not to say that your faith will never ebb or that you will never again go through difficult times. As long as you are in this present world, you will experience good times and hard times. Problems are a necessary part of life, but your connection with Me and your faith in My love and promises can make all the difference in the world!

God's promises stand

The Bible records how I told My disciples that every hair of their heads was counted and that not one sparrow falls to the ground without My Father knowing about it. I told them that they didn't need to worry about their material needs, that if they trusted and followed Me, I would make sure their needs were met.

This may sound unrealistic in today's materialistic world, where the pursuit of money seems more important than ever. Times have changed, but My promises haven't. They are just as sure today as they were 2,000 years ago. Seek first the kingdom of God and obey His Word to the best of your ability, and My Father will provide everything you need (Matthew 6:33; Psalm 84:11).

When you love Me and are trying to follow My example of loving and caring for others, God will take care of you. He is a father who makes sure his children's needs are met. That doesn't mean, though, that you can expect a life of nothing but luxury and ease. The tough times are also part of your heavenly Father's plan to shape your character. And just like an earthly father doesn't automatically give his children everything they want, God doesn't necessarily give you everything you want. He gives you what you need and what He knows is best for you—not only best for your body, but more importantly for your immortal spirit.

How to be happy when times are tough

When money is scarce, your faith in My ability to supply for you is often tested. Voices of discouragement tell you that My promises aren't true, that I won't supply for you as I said I would. But don't succumb to those doubts, because in the end I will come through for you if you do your best to follow what I have said. Sometimes I answer immediately, but other times it takes awhile.

Many factors affect My ability to answer your prayers and provide for you, including the choices that you and others make, so don't become discouraged or impatient or think I don't care or won't supply. Sometimes you and I both have to wait till all the conditions are right.

In the meantime, count your blessings. Thank Me for those things I've already given you, things that are to be treasured above material comforts, things that money can't buy: the love of those dearest to you, true friendships, peace of heart and mind, and the fulfillment and satisfaction that comes from knowing and loving Me. Value those things above all, and you'll have the key to happiness and My spiritual blessings, no matter what your material circumstances may be.

Give and you will receive

If you put your trust in the economies and financial institutions of this world, or if you think worldly financial schemes will bring you happiness, you're doomed to disappointment. That's because those systems are based on selfishness, and selfishness ultimately leads to unhappiness. Even if you achieve financial success by those means, as a few do, you will never be truly happy knowing that your success came at the expense of others.

How much better to trust Me and do things My way! My financial plan is based on love, cooperation, fairness, unselfishness, and sharing. It's the direct opposite of me-first worldly economics. That may not make sense in financial terms, but it does in terms of My blessings.

Share with others, even if you don't have much yourself. That's the simple secret to receiving My blessings, both material and spiritual: Give and I will give to you (Luke 6:38). Those who give unselfishly will be rewarded with more, but those who hold back from helping others when they could, for fear of not having enough for themselves, cut themselves off from the blessings I have waiting for them if only they would give (Proverbs 11:24–25).

Give unselfishly of yourself and your resources, and I will more than repay. The quicker you demonstrate your faith in Me and My promises by giving from what you have, the quicker I can start blessing you with more.

Better than money in the bank

The richest man in the world is the one who has faith. He could lose every material thing he possesses and still be happy. Faith is better than money in the bank to the person who has it and puts it to use.

I fed over 5,000 people from only five small loaves of bread and two fish, I turned water into wine, and I healed a woman who had spent all she had on doctors and medicine, to no avail (Matthew 14:15–21; John 2:1–10; Mark 5:25–29). I also healed hundreds of others who were completely beyond medical help and performed many other miracles that all the money in the world couldn't buy.

And I can do miracles for you—whatever you need. I am alive and well and able to supply all your needs. I'm just waiting for you to ask, so reach out with the hand of faith and receive.

When life is just plain hard

The crafting process

I am like a sculptor and you are like the marble. A block of marble may not look like much or be worth much in its rough form, but it has potential. It takes quite a bit of hammering and chiseling to create a thing of beauty from that piece of rock. The chisel is sharp, the blows are hard, and it's not an altogether pleasant process for the marble, but the finished product is worth it.

No one benefits much from easy times. Such times are enjoyable and everyone wishes they could last forever, but they don't contribute much to one's character. So when troubles come into your life, don't be discouraged or resentful. Instead, know that I have allowed them for a reason: to work My good purpose. My hand is crafting you into a thing of beauty. It is hard to imagine this when you are a work in progress, but faith in Me can give you the grace to endure.

Faith will see you through the crafting process, and when the Sculptor's work is done, you and I will behold and be pleased with the result—My masterpiece, the thing of beauty that is your life.

Seasons of life

When you hit bottom, when dreams give way to disappointment, when all you've worked so hard for goes to pieces, when life no longer holds any purpose or promise, you are tempted to despair and wonder if there is any reason to go on living. In extreme situations you may even be tempted to end it all yourself, right now.

That's when you must remember that you were created for a purpose, and that purpose isn't a single, one-time thing; it's multifaceted and complex. As long as you live, there will be something more you can accomplish—something you are meant to accomplish—and there is always more to get out of life. The end of one dream doesn't mean the end of all dreams. Just as the seasons come and go in their cycle, periods of success or setback, fulfillment or disappointment, and emotional highs and lows come and go. You may be in the depths of despair now, but that won't last forever.

Soon you will find hope and a reason to go on—and the sooner you ask Me to show you what I have for you next, the sooner you will find new inspiration and purpose. The best may be just around the corner, but you'll never know if you stop here. Take My hand and let Me lead you into a new season of fruitfulness and fulfillment.

FROM JESUS WITH LOVE—FOR TROUBLED TIMES

Steppingstones

I don't want you to look at your troubles as punishment for your sins, because that is usually not My intent or their true purpose. I do allow troubles sometimes, but always to accomplish something good in your life. Even when you bring on those troubles through your own mistakes or sins, I want you to use them as steppingstones to take you to higher ground. I want each one to bring you a step closer to Me.

Troubles show you that you aren't sufficient in yourself. They make you realize your need for Me and help you learn to depend on Me. As you trust Me through difficult times, you will grow in faith, you will better understand My Word and wise and loving ways, and you will feel My love and come to know Me in a deeper and more personal way than you ever could otherwise.

One day you will be able to look at troubles and trials and see them as needed steppingstones. You will see then that they were the only way to get you to the special place I have for you, near to My heart.

The climb to victory

The rugged climb doesn't dissuade the determined mountain climber; he revels in the challenge. Nothing can stop him from pressing on until he reaches his goal. No adversity can cause him to turn back. When he looks at the steep cliffs ahead, he doesn't focus on the danger but on the toeholds and narrow rock ledges that will take him to the peak. He isn't held back by the harshness of his surroundings or the toll the climb is taking on his body; he is propelled onward and upward by the thought of triumph.

There are many obstacles to surmount in life, but each one you conquer is another one behind you. When the going gets tough, lean on Me. Let Me lead the way and guide you up the rugged cliffs. I know all the danger spots and how to get past them. Together we will surmount each obstacle, together we will reach the summit, and together we will plant the flag of victory. Follow Me!

FROM JESUS WITH LOVE—FOR TROUBLED TIMES

Blessings from burdens

Life has taken an unexpected turn. The road you've been traveling suddenly seems filled with potholes and obstacles. What happened to that smooth pavement you once enjoyed? You awake each day hoping that things will change, but the former good times are just memories. What you're going through is tough, but in My heavenly love and wisdom I'm not going to take these troubles away—not just yet. I will do something even better for you, though.

I want to show you how the burdens you've been carrying are blessings in disguise. I know that's hard to believe, but it's true. Those burdens have weighed on you so heavily that all you could do was look down at the road and sigh, but I can help you turn those weights into wings that will carry you forward.

Bring each burden to Me. Let Me lift them off you, and then come to My arms and let Me renew your spirit. I give perfect peace and love to those who bring their cares to Me. "Come to Me, all you who labor and are heavy laden, and I will give you rest" (Matthew 11:28).

Ever-present help

You can find comfort in knowing that good can come of anything and that I allow trials in your life not to make you miserable, but better. Still, at times it is hard to be so philosophical—all you want is some relief! You don't want to hear, "All this is for your good"—you just want to be free of the problem.

I know how you feel. When I was on the cross, the pain was so excruciating that I just wanted it to be over. I kept reminding Myself that I was enduring this so that you and a whole world full of sinners like you could be brought to salvation. I knew it was worth it, but it was a supreme struggle to keep such altruistic thoughts foremost in My mind. In My Father's time the suffering did cease and I was released into the spiritual realm where such agony could no longer touch Me, but what an ordeal that was!

At the time of My suffering, My Father could not intervene. I had to go through that for you. But now that I have, I am always there to help you through your times of pain and suffering. I let Myself be separated from divine help for that time so you could always have it available. So hold on. The victory, comfort, and surcease from suffering will come.

FROM JESUS WITH LOVE—FOR TROUBLED TIMES

In My time

Why do you have so many problems and so few solutions? And why does it seem that I don't answer your prayers for help? Is something wrong with you? No, My child, it's not like that. I do allow you to have some problems in the hope that they will cause you to turn to Me, but I have the answer to every one and I will work them out eventually.

I know it's hard to wait, but sometimes, for any of a number of reasons, it takes a while for Me to work. Maybe I'm waiting on you to ask Me what you can do to set things in motion. Maybe I'm working in others' hearts to get them to do the right thing. Maybe I'm waiting for other conditions to be right.

It might take time, but in the meantime, if you look to Me for help and ask Me to show you how I see things, I will give you peace of mind and the comfort of My love. I will relieve the pressure.

So don't give up when, even after you have prayed, things don't change right away. Have faith in My love and power to do the impossible. All things are possible if you believe (Mark 9:23). Keep trusting and you will see the answer to your prayers in My time.

Stressed?

Passage to freedom

When life feels like a tiny, windowless room and its four walls are closing in, you can create a window of escape through the Word of God.

As you read and meditate on the Word, as you believe My promises and claim them as your own, you open a window to the spiritual realm where wonderful things await you. The warm sunshine of My love will melt away the tension. Like a breath of fresh air, the soft breeze of My Spirit will clear your mind. Crystal-clear steams of truth and pools of wisdom will refresh your spirit and mind. New vistas will open before you. You will see things from the heavenly perspective and thrill to the new possibilities and challenges before you. You will find new faith and inspiration. That stifled feeling will give way to exhilaration and a passion for living. "The words that I speak to you are spirit, and they are life" (John 6:63).

Learn to turn to the Word when you feel bottled up, and My Word will set you free (John 8:31–32).

Double blessing

Although I have the power to solve your problems instantly, what you sometimes need most is not a quick fix but a wise counselor. I can be that to you.

Quick fixes are nice because they relieve the situation for the moment, but often the gain is only momentary. When solutions come easily, it's easy to take them for granted and not learn from them, so the problems recur. Sometimes you're not meant to go around your problems but through them, because struggles bring with them valuable lessons that strengthen your spirit and make you wiser. You are then better equipped to handle problems that come up later.

How and when I work on your behalf is for Me to decide, but if you're after My best and are trying to learn from every problem situation, you will be doubly blessed in the end. I will fix the problem in My time and My way, and you will be wiser for it.

Stay simple

I spoke great truths, profound words that changed lives and continue to do so. But I also spoke to the children. I was simple, I was clear, and I didn't lose My appreciation of little things. I stopped to enjoy the flowers. I cooked for My disciples.

It's when you can't find joy in the everyday things of life that you become complicated and lose the human touch. You exchange depth of character for a labyrinth of complex thinking, a heart that is sensitive to the things of the spirit for mere head knowledge.

Simplicity is a gift. Everyone starts out with it, but as some people grow up they discount this gift because they associate it with ignorance, naiveté, immaturity, and a lack of sophistication. They prefer to weave a web of complexity to cover it. But did I not say that unless you have childlike simplicity to believe in the "impossible" and the unseen—Me, the One who died for you and rose to life again so you could have the wonderful but simple gift of eternal life—you cannot enter the kingdom of Heaven? The gift of simplicity remains for those who have the humility and wisdom to value it and claim it as their own.

There is much to discover throughout life and even more in Heaven, but you will always find that the most profound truths, the greatest beauty, and the most outstanding wisdom are expressed simply.

Taking back control

There's so much that you need to do each day, so much that you want to do, and so much that others expect of you. You feel pulled in all directions. Pressure. Tension. Anxiety. Will it ever stop?

It won't stop on its own, but you can break the cycle. You don't have to remain entangled in the unending struggle to do more and have more. Life doesn't have to be a daily crisis. You don't have to be the prisoner of unrealistic expectations. Let Me help you regain control of your life.

The root of the problem is simple: You try to do too much, more than is humanly possible, and you put your mind, body, and spirit under pressure they were never meant to handle. It's time to reassess. Determine what things mean the most to you—your primary long-term goals and responsibilities—and what other things are essential to achieve those things. Channel your energies into those things, and let go of the rest. Once you've done this, the pressures that once seemed unbearable will start to dissipate.

Do you want a new lease on life? You can have one, but you have to be willing to let go of the pressures that drive your present one. It's up to you.

When the burden gets too heavy

You're right—it's all too much at times! The problems are too big, the pressures too much, the tasks too hard, the burdens too heavy. It is all too much for your frail human frame, but it's never too much for Me. Give it all to Me. That's the secret; that's the solution.

Cast your cares on Me. Lay your burdens at My feet and leave them there. Don't pick them up and walk off with them again. Leave them for Me to take care of as only I can.

As you look to Me and lean on Me, I will take over and do what you couldn't do on your own. Even seemingly impossible situations are simple to Me. Sometimes I will solve the problem without your getting involved or even knowing how I did it. Sometimes I will send others to help you. Sometimes I will work in others' hearts. Sometimes I will give you solutions so you can help fix the problem yourself. I work in lots of ways, depending on the situation and the need. As you learn to bring your problems to Me and ask Me to work on your behalf, I will. That's a promise!

Regrets

Outstretched arms of forgiveness

You're bound to make wrong choices sometimes because you're human, but I still love you. If I were to love only, perfect people, there wouldn't be anyone for Me to love because everyone falls short at times (Romans 3:23). There is no one who gets it all right. I don't ask or expect perfection of you.

It saddens Me when you willfully do wrong, but I don't hold it against you if you are sincerely sorry. Instead, I extend My arms in forgiveness and draw you close to Me. My forgiveness is a manifestation of My love for you.

Depending on the situation, you may still have to live with the consequences of your wrongdoing, but once you ask Me for forgiveness, I forgive. It's that simple! From that moment on, I don't even remember your sin (1 John 1:9; Hebrews 8:12). As high as the heavens are above the earth, so great are My mercies toward you (Psalm 103:11). I erase the sins of the past and offer you a new start (Psalm 51:1).

Where you go from there is up to you. It largely depends on your desire to change and your determination to leave behind the things of the past so you can move forward in My love. Though you fall, I will always be there to pick you up. My loving help, like My forgiveness, is endless.

If only…

Sometimes you feel that if only you could turn back time, retrace your steps, and undo mistakes, things would be so much better. If only you could apply what you know now to past situations, you could reverse painful experiences and possibly change the course of your life. But the truth is, those situations—mistakes included—are what have made you the person you are today. The most painful and trying circumstances were the ones that gave you the most strength and maturity. Through your mistakes you have learned invaluable lessons. Mistakes also help you to be more humble and therefore more loving, and that makes you more useful to Me and easier for others to live with.

If you were able to travel back in time and change some of your decisions and actions, you would very likely be unhappy with the results. You wouldn't have nearly as much depth of character as you do today. So instead of regretting the past, be thankful for what it has taught you.

Admit your need

I see into your heart and know your regrets. I long to release you from their weight and take away the pain and hurt they cause you. But first you need to give them to Me; you need to ask for help.

I help those who admit they need Me. So don't try to hide the hurt in your heart from Me or yourself. Don't try to pretend it's not there, and don't think that I will think any less of you for it. I already know everything about you, and it doesn't change My love for you one iota.

You feel you deserve to bear the load of guilt and remorse that you do, but that's not the way it's meant to be. You've made mistakes, but I died for the express purpose of lifting the responsibility for your mistakes and sins from your shoulders. Ask Me to forgive you, and I will both forgive you and free you from that weight.

Forgive and forget

My heart aches to see the heartache you have felt, for I feel the pain, the anger, the regret, the remorse, the feelings of being hurt and angered by the faults and mistakes and even the sins of others. I also know that it's human nature to want to retaliate, to want revenge, and to fight against forgiving and burying your differences. To truly forgive and forget is one of the most difficult things for anyone.

Only through Me can you be freed from these roots of bitterness that entangle your heart. I am love, I am forgiveness, and I'm here for you, waiting to lift this load of bitterness that you've been carrying around. Take it off and give it to Me. Just say, "Jesus, take this. I don't want it anymore." I will make it disappear forever. Together we will bury it in My love, so that you can once again feel the brightness and lightness of My love and the happy joy of My Spirit. I will make you whole again.

Start anew today

Life is all about the little decisions you make every day. Decisions of the past have had their effect, but every new day can be a new start. No matter what has happened up till now, you have a chance to make the right decisions today.

Don't waste time reliving the pain of past mistakes and wrong decisions. That only saps your power to do what you can do today. You can't change the past, but the future is what you make it, starting right now, so take full advantage of the present.

Learn from past mistakes and put them behind you today. Forgive those who have wronged you and ask forgiveness from those you have wronged. That probably won't be easy, but don't put it off.—Do it today. Look to Me and My Word for fresh courage and hope, starting today. Dream new dreams today. Set new goals today. Spend your time on things that truly count today. Love your family today. Be a friend today. Do things better, starting today.

With My help, your future can be filled with wonderful accomplishment and fulfillment that will more than make up for past disappointments—and it all starts today.

Troubles at home

Home of hearts

Marriage brings with it some of the deepest joys you'll ever know, but also some of the greatest challenges. You're building a home of hearts, and if it's going to last it must be built on a solid foundation, beam upon beam, brick upon brick. It's hard work getting everything to fit together properly. After all, no matter how much you love each other, you are two different people and are bound to have some different likes, dislikes, views, and opinions.

It takes a great deal of communication, love, understanding, wisdom, and prayer to build a successful marriage. There will be difficulties and setbacks, but don't let them halt your construction project. The results will be well worth the effort, tears, and troubles you experience along the way. In fact, it is those very troubles that will help you grow closer if you approach them positively, believing that I am able to see you through them. The low points aren't meant to diminish your love, but to bring you even closer. Each time you overcome an obstacle with love and prayer, you strengthen your home of hearts.

Marriage is give and take, joy and tears, talking and listening, forgiving and asking forgiveness, experiencing good times and not-so-good times. It's remembering the good and choosing to forget the bad.

Parenting through prayer

It's not easy raising children in today's world. Many of the godly values that you want to encourage in your children are constantly being attacked by others who are going the opposite direction. You worry that even your best efforts will fail and that your children will turn their backs on the values you hold dear. I know you're sometimes tempted to give up, but don't. Your concern and care are not in vain.

There's only so much that you can do, even though you try your best. But I'm capable of doing much more than you ever could, and I am here to help. I also understand your children even better than you do, and I know how to best handle their problems. I want to work with you to shape your children into the godly people we both want them to become.

Commit your children to Me in prayer. Through prayer you can be the better parent you want to be. Through prayer you can help protect your children from harm and unwholesome influences. Through prayer you can find My solutions to their problems. Through your prayers I can do what you can't do.

Set aside time each day to pray for your children. Each time you're faced with a troublesome issue, ask Me for the answer. Start today to be a better parent through prayer. Changes that you haven't thought possible will come to pass through the power of prayer.

Breaking the bands of addiction

Having a loved one who is caught in the trap of substance abuse can be one of the most heartbreaking and trying experiences, not only because it's so harmful and dangerous, but also because it's an ongoing problem. It tears you apart to watch someone you love so dearly destroying himself. You've tried to talk sense into him, you've tried to give advice, you've tried to understand what brought this on, you've tried to be patient, and you've tried to be firm. Still, it seems that nothing has helped. That's because, as badly as you want to, you can't solve the problem. Ultimately that's up to him. If he's willing to change, I can break the bands of addiction and heal his body, mind, and spirit, but even I can't override his decisions.

I can, however, work in his heart and mind to help him start making better decisions that will lead to recovery, and this is where you come in. You can help Me work more effectively by praying for him. Until his will is pulling in the right direction, you have to do some of the pulling for him through prayer. Until he is ready to ask for My help himself, you have to ask for My help.

Prayer can work wonders in even the most "impossible" cases, so keep on praying. It may take time, but one day you will see the evidence of My hand at work and your prayers for your dear one being answered. Where there is life, there is hope!

If you've been hurt

Come into My arms now. These arms will never harm you. These arms will never hurt you. These arms are here to protect you. These arms are strong to guard, yet gentle to soothe and heal. These arms will keep on loving you no matter what. I'm sorry you've been treated badly, and I want to heal your hurts. I want to give you the loving care you desire and deserve.

My love is always there for you. As you come to Me and let Me be your true Love, I will take care of you. You will never be disappointed in Me. I will provide the comfort and love you need as you draw closer through prayer, reading My Word, and listening to My whispers of love and reassurance in your heart. Come and find peace and your heart's desires in Me. I love you, My sweet one, and never want to see you hurt. Earthly loves may fail you, but My love never fails. Come into My arms now. There you will find the love and understanding you have longed for.

Harmful relationships

Sometimes it's best to ride out domestic problems; sometimes it's best to distance yourself from them for a time; sometimes it's best to get help from a friend, relative, or professional; and sometimes it's best to move on. It's often humanly impossible to reason these things out or know which way to go because there are so many factors and emotions involved, but if you ask Me, I will show you what's best. I will also give you the strength to do what I show you is best.

Love, humility, prayer, and forgiveness can overcome any problem, but it takes two. If you have done your part but the abusive relationship continues, then it's time to get out. You should be loving and patient and forgive, but you must not continue to put yourself in danger.

If I show you that it is best to make a break with the past and start anew, I will also give you the courage to see it through. I can set you on a new course where you will be happy and safe. I can even send a new romantic love your way—one who will be gentle and caring and help you overcome the hurts of the past.

So if you find yourself caught in a tangled web of emotions, if you are being hurt yet can't pull yourself free, ask Me to help you and I will. I have your best interests at heart and will provide the very best for you.

Close the door to the past

Time heals all things—even a broken heart. The hurt and anger you feel now will fade with time, but it will be much quicker and easier to bear if you ask Me to help you. It may still take longer than you'd like, but slow healing is often the best kind.

At the same time, you must do your part. Don't hang onto the past. Don't refuse to be healed. Let go of the anger and bitterness. Let it all go. As difficult as it may be, you must accept what has happened and forgive. Only then will you be able to close the door on the past, find relief from the painful memories, and get on with life.

At times like this when your whole world seems to be falling apart, when things so dear to you have been taken away, you may wonder if I still love and care for you. The answer to that is simple—yes! More than ever I want to show you just how much I love you! Your life is emptier now, but I'm wanting and waiting to fill that void with My love. So go ahead—go through and close the door on the past. I'm on the other side of the door and have a lot of love and other good things in store for you.

When

loved ones

pass on

Preparation for passing

I know how difficult it is for you to see your loved one suffer day after day, and to watch her strength and very life fade. It's not only difficult to see her in pain, but you're also faced with the reality that she probably won't be with you much longer, and it's hard to think about what your future will be like without her.

Though your loved one suffers physically, her spirit is being prepared for a new and far better life in Heaven. I am putting My peace within her and bringing her to a fuller understanding of My will and plan.

This peace and understanding is there for you too. Ask Me for faith and grace for each day, each hour, each moment. If you do that, I will give both you and your loved one all the spiritual resources you need. Though it is difficult, this time of suffering can also bring about beautiful things in the spirit. You can be closer to each other and to Me than you ever have been before.

Keep interceding for your loved one in prayer. Continue to be supportive, reassuring, and do everything you can to lift her spirits. And do not fear—I am with you both.

New beginning

Your loved one has not vanished like smoke in the wind. He has merely passed on to a new place, a new existence.

His love for you is just as strong as ever. The memories he shared with you are just as fresh in his mind and remembered even more fondly. The pain you suffered together is still there too, but now he understands what it was all for, and he accepts it.

Now you must accept it as well. You must believe that this end of his earthly life was not meant to be the end for you. He is still living, only in another realm. He is still fulfilling the purpose for which he was created, and so must you.

When the time comes for you, too, to pass from the shadows into the light, you will better understand. Then the love that you had to let go of will be with you once again. It will be the beginning of a whole new and wonderful life of love that you will share for all eternity.

In My arms

Though hearts break and tears flow on earth, in Heaven there is rejoicing because this dear child of Mine is in My arms, perfectly happy and perfectly whole. Here I am able to hold him close, wipe away his tears, and show him My love. Oh, how great that love is!

In just a little while you will be reunited. Until then, hold tightly to My hand and let Me comfort you. Remember that the one whom you love but see no more is now in a better place. He is in My presence, where he is free from all pain and problems and experiences My love without measure.

You cannot possibly imagine the love and joy and freedom that your loved one now experiences in the heavenly realm, but I can give you a little foretaste—a little glimpse of Heaven and its wonders. Won't you come into My arms and experience a touch of that love? Let Me hold you close. Let Me wipe away your tears. Let Me ease your pain and mend your broken heart. Let Me carry you through this time of heartbreak and loss. Come, find sweet relief in My arms, just as your loved one has.

The journey to love

Your loved one isn't lost to you forever. She has just stepped into a different dimension. It's as though she's gone on a journey ahead of you, and one day you'll join her in that new world. It's a beautiful world, full of splendor and happiness, joy and laughter, peace and plenty—a place where dreams become reality.

I know you're sad and sorely miss her, but please be happy for her. She's been freed from pain and found perfect love and perfect peace in Me. Though you'll have to walk the road of life without her for a time, this time apart will make your reunion in Heaven all the sweeter.

Love doesn't die when a soul passes from this earth to the realm beyond. Love lives forever. Love joins hearts and transcends the boundaries that separate your worlds. Her love is a treasure you'll never lose, and so is Mine. I will comfort your heart and give you peace until the day you finish your journey and find yourself in the arms of your loved one once again.

Let the healing begin

Hers was a senseless death and not her fault. She was just in the wrong place at the wrong time. Now she's gone with no warning and no goodbyes. I know the questions you struggle with now. I know the sorrow you feel, and My heart breaks for you.

I also understand how you feel that nothing could ever compensate for your loss, yet you long for retribution; you want justice to be served. That is a natural reaction, but it won't bring your loved one back. If you seek revenge or harbor resentment, it will slowly poison your own spirit. As impossible as this may seem, as unrealistic as this may sound, the best thing you can do at this moment is forgive from your heart the one responsible. This takes the kind of forgiveness I was talking about when I told My disciples, "Love your enemies and pray for those who spitefully use you, that you may be sons of your Father in Heaven" (Matthew 5:44–45).

Justice will run its course, if not in this life then in the next, but what I want you to do now is forgive. Only then will you be freed from the shackles of bitterness and only then will the emotional healing begin. I will help you if you will try.

Peace that surpasses understanding

It's hard to lose loved ones, I know. Even if you believe that they're safe and secure in Heaven, that they have joined Me, and that I watch over them lovingly, you still feel the loss. But I want to comfort you. If you will let Me, I can fill that void with love and perfect peace—peace that transcends your natural reasoning and emotions, peace that doesn't make sense in the way you usually try to make sense of things, but is wonderfully real and wonderfully comforting.

The Bible talks about a "peace that surpasses all understanding" (Philippians 4:7). This is the kind of comfort that I can give. Even when you have every reason to sorrow and despair, I can pour My soothing balm over your spirit. I can pick up the pieces of your broken heart and put it back together again. You will always love and miss the one you lost, but you don't need to feel alone or unloved or despair over your loss. I am here for you.

Comfort from the realm beyond

The only sadness that could possibly spoil the joy of those who come home to Me is that of seeing loved ones grieving and finding no comfort. Your beloved wants to reach out and comfort you now, and he can within certain limits.

He has left the physical plane, but he is still very much alive in the spiritual one. He is still himself, he still loves you, he still feels your love, and it is possible for you to still feel his love, too. He still wants to be a part of your life—not only through your memories, but also through his spiritual presence. Just as My Spirit is ever present and you can hear My voice from the spiritual realm, so is the spirit of your loved one alive and so is he able to touch you from this realm.

Your spirits are still connected. Those times when you feel him near, when you sense his presence and can almost hear his voice or think his thoughts, that's because he is near. I've created a means by which you can remain connected with your loved one in spirit. He continues to watch over you from the realm beyond.

Why?

"Where are You?"

When things go wrong it's easy to ask, "Jesus, where are You when I need You?" It seems that I have failed you or that My love and patience have run out.

At times like that your faith is being tested, and when you react in doubt rather than faith, you limit My ability to help you. It can become a vicious cycle.

Yet there are some people who remain positive, no matter what their circumstances. How can they face disappointment and even disaster so calmly? It's because they have strong faith in My love and the promises I've made in My Word. It's because they have sought and found a close personal link with Me. It's because they have learned to turn to Me in their times of need. It's not that their faith is never tested, but they know where to turn to for the help they need to pass the test.

Here's the secret to that kind of victory: Prepare for the hard times by learning to stay close to Me when times are good. Make a point of looking for My loving hand at work around you. Count your blessings. Cultivate an attitude of faith and trust and thankfulness. Then when the going gets rough, you will know I'm only a prayer away.

Is life fair?

Why is it that so often those who are loving, kind, and unselfish suffer, while those who only look out for themselves, dash the dreams of others to get what they want, and trample others in their charge up the ladder of success seem to have it better? Isn't life unfair in that way? Shouldn't right living be rewarded and wrongdoing be punished? Yes, that's the way it should be, and one day it will. Justice will come in the next life.

Judgment will be meted out to those who were unloving and cruel and caused others to suffer; they will have to suffer the consequences of their evil actions until they learn the error of their ways and repent. But when those who lived right pass on, although they may have suffered or gone without on earth, they will be blessed with greater rewards and joy than they ever imagined.

And besides being rewarded in the next life, I bless the loving and unselfish in this life—often in ways that can't be measured in dollars and cents, though. I bless them spiritually. I bless them with happiness and contentment, peace of mind and a clear conscience. Meanwhile, some of the wealthiest people in the world are also some of the saddest, loneliest, and most lost, because money can't satisfy the needs of the spirit.

So pursue the blessings of My Spirit— the love, joy, contentment, and feeling of fulfillment that comes only from knowing that you've done your best to lead a godly life. Only then will you truly appreciate that life is fair.

Do I care?

When you see, read, and hear about so much pain and suffering around you, it's easy to question why I allow such troubles in the world. Don't I care? Yes, I do! My heart breaks for those who suffer, especially for those who lose loved ones or livelihood or their own health and happiness because of man's inhumanity to man. I am deeply saddened by much of what I see happening in the world today.

It is only natural to question: "Why, then, don't You put an end to all that evil now?" As much as I abhor evil, I have to let humanity continue on its course. People were created with free will, and I must let them exercise that free will, to choose to do good or evil. My justice isn't always executed immediately, but it is eventually, either in this life or the next. I have to let things run their course on earth, according to people's choices. At present it seems that evil is gaining the upper hand, but rest assured that ultimately love will win out and the world will be changed. All will be made right in the end, because I am both loving and just.

It's not God's fault!

God, My Father, is not to blame for all the pain, death, heartache, and suffering in the world. The truth is, most of the world's ills are caused by people's selfish and destructive attitudes and actions.

Take war, for example, or poverty. God is not to blame for either. He created the world with enough resources for all to have plenty if they would live in love and peace and harmony and cooperation as He intended. But instead, man's selfishness, greed, pride, and competitive spirit have created a very different world where people and whole nations deprive and destroy each other for momentary superiority and selfish gain.

Science is another culprit. While modern science and technology have brought many wonderful benefits, they have also created new perils. If God were to let things go on much longer as they are, mankind would destroy itself—if not through nuclear bombs or chemical or germ warfare or some scientific experiment gone horribly wrong, then by short-sighted exploitation of the world's resources and destruction of the environment.

It's not a pretty picture, but it's about to change. God will not let mankind destroy itself. Before the world gets to that point, I will return to set things right—and it won't be long!

The promise of Romans 8:28

"We know that all things work together for good to those who love God, to those who are the called according to His purpose" (Romans 8:28). This is My promise to you.

I wish everyone could learn to live in love, but because people are not perfect and they often make selfish choices, I gave that promise as a safeguard to My children who love Me. In this world there will be injustice and selfishness and difficulties and pain, but I have the power to overrule all of that for your sake. No matter what the choices of those around you, I am able to give you what's best for you.

Sometimes what I know is best is different than what you think of as "best." Sometimes My best means more brokenness, more compassion, more understanding of others, more humility. All of these qualities are part of My best in your life.

Of course, I'm not able to turn these bad situations for your good or to bless and reward you in other ways unless you let Me work in your life, but the beauty of this promise is that the moment you fulfill the conditions—loving Me and yielding to My will, My purpose in your life—I begin to work on your behalf. No matter what mess you find yourself in, when you love Me and yield to My purpose in your life, I am able to turn all things for your good.

Prince of Peace

Once, when I was crossing the Sea of Galilee with My disciples, a storm arose and threatened to sink our small boat. My disciples were frightened, but I commanded the storm to cease—"Peace! Be still!"—and the wind and waves obeyed Me. So shall it be one day soon when I say, "Enough!" and cause the storms of wars and strife to cease.

All of the problems of today's world prove that people can't solve their own problems. The world cannot survive without its Savior; it needs Me. Universal, lasting peace is not possible without Me, the Prince of Peace, but the time will come when the whole world will submit to My loving and righteous rule. Just a little longer and I will dry the eyes of the downtrodden and those who have been cruelly tormented by the horrors of war. One day, war will be a thing of the past—a concept only scarcely understood by those living then.

In the meantime, you can have real and lasting peace in your heart—peace that can withstand anything—by receiving Me as your personal Savior and turning to Me, the Prince of Peace, in your time of need. I will always be there for you.

Keep your eyes on Heaven

When you and those you love suffer unjustly, that's when it's more important than ever to hold on to your faith, lest the sadness of the world settle on your heart. The assurance of a better world to come will see you through even the darkest days.

Keep your eyes on your eternal home in Heaven—that wonderful place where you will be reunited with those you love and where all will be love and light and joy and happiness. You will know then that it was worth it all, for on that day the sacrifices and pain of separation from those you love will be erased.

If it's hard for you to have that kind of faith, ask Me to help you see things as I do. Ask Me to show you what I have in store for you and your loved ones in Heaven, and I will. I do this so that you may be encouraged and find the strength to bear the troubles of the present. I am not able to reveal all that I have prepared for you, but I can reveal some of it to you now (1 Corinthians 2:9–10). Keep your eyes on Heaven and the troubles of this present world will seem small by comparison—and they are.

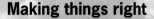

Making things right

Life is a great cycle of cause and effect. Everyone makes choices every day, and everyone's choices affect others. The combination of everyone's choices and the effect those choices have on others makes the world what it is.

Every problem can be traced to some unloving or selfish choice someone made. These sins are the major cause of problems in the world today: selfishness and lack of love. People either don't see how their wrong choices affect others, or they don't care enough to do things differently.

You may feel that the world is too messed up, that too many wrong choices have been made, that it doesn't matter much what you do, that it's hopeless. But that's not true. Just as every problem can be traced to a wrong decision, every solution begins with a wise and loving decision to do the right thing, the loving and unselfish thing.

A little bit of love can make a lot of difference. One act of kindness or unselfishness can start a whole chain reaction of events that will, in the long run, make life a lot better for a lot of people. So don't despair because there is so much suffering and grief and wrong in the world. Instead, do what you can to make things right and encourage others to do the same. The world won't change in a day, but you can make a difference if you try.

Afterword

If you haven't yet experienced the kind of love expressed in these messages from Jesus, it may be that you haven't yet received His gifts of eternal love and life by accepting Him as your Savior. Jesus won't force Himself on you. He waits humbly for you to invite Him into your life. He says, "Behold, I stand at the door [of your heart] and knock. If anyone hears My voice and opens the door, I will come in" (Revelation 3:20). You can receive Him right now by sincerely praying the following:

Dear Jesus, thank You for dying for me so I can have eternal life. Please forgive me now for every wrong and unloving thing I have ever done. Wash away all that, and help me to do better. I need Your love to fill and satisfy my heart. I want the life of heavenly happiness You have for me—here and now, and in Heaven hereafter. I open the door of my heart and ask You, Jesus, to come in. Thank You for hearing and answering my prayer. Amen.